Carry On Keeping On

Karen Parry

Published by New Generation Publishing in 2021

First Edition

ISBN 978-1-80031-295-1

www.newgeneration-publishing.com

New Generation Publishing

Acknowledgements

I feel that in order for me to have been able to write this book it would not have been possible without life's experiences and the people in my life to share them with.

I have a great lot of love, respect and gratitude for many people in my life including my family and friends. We learn from our experiences, feelings and emotions and through the highs and lows that take us through our life.

I was blessed to have a solid and stable upbringing with loving and caring parents and an older sister. My parents fostered teenagers so I was fortunate to share this experience and valued my childhood even more so, in realisation of how lucky I was and awakened to the harsh realities that not every child was blessed with the same start in life as myself. I learnt from these kids that through resilience and hope, despite any challenge they had in their life, they couldn't change their past but they could shape the future they desired with the help of those that were put on their paths to aid their life's choices for the better.

I have been blessed with many special friendships in my life to help complete it. And look forward to many more that stumble across my path in my future.

I have too many special friends and family to mention all of them, but I would like to make a dedication to some special friends that I was close to that have passed to spirit over the last few years. Tony Wood was a special friend who would go out of his way to do anything for me. I loved him dearly and will always treasure his friendship and help that he gave to me. Peter Wilson who was my teacher and working partner of demonstrating mediumship. He became a very special friend of mine and I feel blessed to have had both of them in my life. When I started on my spiritual path I would say I owe a lot of gratitude and respect to my late friend Liz, she opened the door to the part of myself that I was still yet to discover and was a special part of my life for many years.

I would also like to dedicate this book to both my nan and dad who have passed to spirit. I love and miss them both dearly. Some of the philosophies that are included in this book were inspired after my nan's passing and I felt that she was around me at that time with words of comfort to help me grieve her loss. My dad was an inspiration and very funny, no matter what life threw at him, he never lost his spirit and smile and I hope to carry some of his joy and strength within me, in my lifetime. I have to say a huge thank you to my sister and brother in law who kept me sane through the first lockdown in 2020, they invited me in to their home to stay and share the daunting time that we all found ourselves faced with. Lastly and most importantly, I'd like to acknowledge my eternal gratitude to my mum, who remains to be my rock and support, always and forever.

Introduction About this Book

These poems, philosophies and meditations were inspired in 2020 during the period of the Covid-19 pandemic, life changed for us all with uncertain times ahead. I had time to reflect on my life during this time since, like many, I was forced to stop working. I reassessed what I wanted to continue in my life and thought about what I wasn't happy with and what needed to change. I felt during this time lockdown would probably have had the same effect on many others that were forced into the same situation as myself. Many carried on working and putting themselves at risk, working on the front line to help others in need such as carers and the NHS, and all keyworkers who continued to keep our country and other countries going with supplies and essential services.

I'd like to think that during this time people reached out to one another, volunteers and people working together as a community to look after each other and offer a helping hand where it was needed. Within these times of struggle we were each given the opportunity to respond in the way we felt necessary. I personally used this time as an opportunity to use previous writings and create new ones and put my work into the form of a book with a mixture of poems, philosophies, quotes and meditations. This gave me focus, something to keep my mind from the stress and worries of the time that we were going through. I am happy to be able to share some guidance and upliftment with you and I hope that you enjoy my book.

Contents

Connecting with Mother Earth Poem

In my own space, where time has now stopped,
my mind slowing down, all troubles forgot.
Away from the crowd, where freedom exists,
as I'm drifting closer into this wonderful bliss.

To be in this stillness and have this heartfelt connection,
with Mother Earth's beauty in its magic creation.
Strength felt from the trees, birds freely fly by,
this peace and serenity brings a tear to my eye.

Surrounded by nature, wildlife and colour,
brings me closer to my spirit and my heart becomes fuller.
With a love felt so deep, intense and so strong,
this feeling inside in which I have longed.

Nature

We go through the varying seasons of the year which illustrate different pictures and scenes, beautiful colours, different skies and weather conditions all of which can alter and affect our inner moods and feelings. When you connect with nature, taking walks and just being at one with the earth, you can gain strength and balance from Mother Earth and its beautiful creation. Noticing the joys from the birds singing, clear blue skies, strength and energy from the trees in the woodlands, feeling connected to the Earth as you walk in peace and harmony.

"Next time you are outdoors amongst nature absorb all what is around you, look more closely to all of this life and what we have to appreciate and be grateful for."

Sky

The sky has many shades. On a bright sunny day it can be sparkling clear blue with no clouds and then there can be days full of clouds and storms, thunder and lighting, this can represent how our moods forever change and how we move through various emotions at times in our life. However the sky appears and whatever life challenges you with, trust that everything will always come back round in full circle.

"After the storm or darkness the sunrise will always appear. So whatever life presents to you await in patience and trust for that clear sparkling sky again."

Life

We are born on a specific date and we die on a specific date, that is a given in life but the part in between is how we spend our life and what we make of it and that is a unique experience that we are granted. Let's embrace life together and always try to remember that we are all connected in some way to another, biological family and our extended family to all that is: the spirit world, friends, neighbours, pets, our teachers and so on. We can be connected to a book we read and feel inspired, to music that we listen to that uplifts and moves us. There is nothing that we are not connected to, be it good, bad or indifferent, we are never alone even in the triumphs and challenges of life.

"Life is a gift, it is down to each individual on how it is used and lived. Will you live in regrets or will you fulfil your potential and live a happy and contented life."

Connecting to the Earth Meditation

- Close your eyes, focus on each breath in and out, let go of worries and tension.
- Imagine yourself in a field surrounded by nature, Mother Earth's beauty, the grass, flowers, trees and so on.
- Find a tree of your choice and sit down with your back against the trunk. Just for a moment take your time to breathe in the healing energies and strength from the tree and build a connection.
- You feel at one with the tree as if it is a part of you, your feet are the roots of the tree, your body becomes the trunk and arms are the branches.
- You feel so strong and powerful now, feeling a sense of enlightenment and empowerment, losing sense of your physical body and becoming one with the earth and nature, just a pure being of light and oneness, filled with love.
- Stay with these feelings until you are ready to return to your waking conscious and open your eyes.

Connecting with the Spirit World

Poem

In this time as we sit in silence, a bond can grow
stronger and deepens the connection.
A blessing from the spirit world, that surrounds us with
love, wisdom, guidance and protection.

Holding us each with a loving embrace, by a strong
vibrant and glowing light.
You come to guide and reassure us, that we can each
achieve our goals in sight.

Your love and encouragement is felt, helping us on our
path and bringing us along.
A sense of tranquillity, peace and hope, always there
when we need to keep strong.

Spirit

We each are spirit not only are those who have journeyed to the "spirit world". The more we can recognise this within each of us, we can then become more in touch with the life force of God that flows through each of us and makes us who we are, our purpose in this life and recognise our value and uniqueness as a gift to the world.

"When you look in the mirror and see your reflection, see the presence of God, because God lives within each of us beneath the physical surface."

Spiritual Development

When we go through our lives we learn more and more and we grow from life's experiences that usually cause us hurt, pain and defeats etc. For without these experiences we would not know how to appreciate the good that we have and grow spiritually within our human existence. We always have the chance to learn from past mistakes by having repeated lessons in life to do and act in the best way possible for the highest good.

"Observe yourself from an outside perspective and try to understand fully the meaning to your life and its occurrences, your actions and keep things in perspective by seeing the bigger picture to any given challenge."

Spirit World

We each are spirit, only in this life we are spirit having a human experience. When we transition to the next stage we become a higher vibration or energy and we continue to evolve. When a loved one passes, although they don't have their physical body any longer, they still have their consciousness and hear our thoughts and prayers in our times of need. They can come and help guide, support and comfort us. Just because we lose someone in physical sight it does not mean we cannot see them in our mind's eye and feel them in our heart.

"Reach out to your loved ones in spirit if you wish to reconnect. Silently and trustingly wait to feel, sense, hear or know their presence in your own individual way that is correct for you."

Connect with Spirit Meditation

- Close your eyes, take a few deep breaths and let go of your thoughts for the day.
- Imagine a staircase in front of you which has ten steps that lead down to a door.
- Count from one to ten internally, as you walk down each step relaxing deeper and deeper with each number.
- As you reach the bottom step you open the door which leads you to a rose quartz crystal cave, as you enter you feel unconditional love, peace and happiness.
- Walk to a seat in the centre of the cave which has enough room for two, as you just sit and be, you think of a loved one that has passed to the spirit world.
- You begin to feel their presence beside you, whether this is in the form of thoughts, visions, a sense or a feeling, your awareness is exactly right for you.
- Spend time to embrace their warmth and love and use this opportunity to have an inward conversation with your loved one.
- Once it is time to leave, make your way back to the door and up the stairs to where you began.

Process of Healing Poem

In the process of healing, problems surface to the top,
before they can be healed, they're felt again before they stop.

To acknowledge, understand and accept, these mixed emotions and these feelings,
is the crisis that you work through, as the breakthrough to your healing.

We have a choice whether to accept help offered, or instead we can shut it out,
we have the choice to believe healing works, rather than hold self-doubt.

Healing

We could be in need of physical healing for ailments and disease but what we need to remember is that our state of mind and emotions influence our physical well-being, so the more we nourish our emotional state of mind, the more our health improves. We can be in need of physical, emotional, mental and spiritual healing. In terms of spiritual healing, this could be to become more in touch with our own spirit, allowing us to feel whole and more complete, and therefore happier.

"Healing doesn't mean cure, it simply means finding inner balance and peace which then reflects on external factors of the self."

Choices

We always have a choice, whatever our current circumstances are, there is no such thing as being stuck. We have the freedom of our minds to choose the thoughts we want which then reflect on our outer world and our happiness. If you have options and are not sure which direction to go in, take a step back, wait patiently and allow your heart to choose.

"Choose wisely with confidence and passion, to keep going forward without hesitation or doubts, the choice you make will always be the right one."

Courage

Sometimes when we have changes and challenges in our life, we have to find that underlying courage to keep us strong and not fearful. Courage is within each of us, we may need to show courage for a loved one if they are in a time of need or it could be for ourselves when we are faced with something that is outside our comfort zone.

"Go within to unleash your strength and courage and bring forth these qualities into your life when called upon."

Healing Rainbow Meditation

- Close your eyes and relax.
- Imagine a rainbow and all the colours.
- You notice the colour red from the rainbow, you breathe in the power and energy from the red colour giving you strength, courage and determination.
- The colour changes to orange, this colour helps to remove any blocks or fears.
- You now feel the colour yellow in your awareness and feel a sense of abundance, happiness and joy.
- This colour then changes to green, as you open your heart allow the energy of green to give you a sense of unconditional love and peace.
- Then you see the colour blue, you feel trust, confidence and serenity.
- You now see the colour indigo to clear your mind and focus more.
- Lastly you see violet and feel completely at one and content and pure.
- All the colours of the rainbow have helped heal you, they fade into the background and you open your eyes and come back.

Be Kind Poem

As we are here on this earth plane together,
let's do our best to be kind to each other.
The world that we live in, with our friends and family,
spread love and kindness with truth and humility.

In times when we are faced with changes and stress,
through your struggles remember there will be someone
with less.
We are all here together, precious moments to share,
live the life of your dreams,
take heart and dare.

With compassion and sincerity be loving to others and
yourself,
happiness with others is worth more than financial
wealth.
So be brave, be happy and kind to yourself too,
lead the best life you can and be proud to be you.

Judgement

Blood is thicker than water, but the spirit is thicker than blood. If we reach out to one another, spirit to spirit, and see each other in this perspective, it may help us to hold less judgement on one another and make room for more compassion and tolerance for human errors and actions. The spirit world and our own spirit does not judge, none of us are perfect but we can try to be a better person than we were yesterday.

"Judgement narrows the minds way of acceptance, embrace unconditional love in your heart and become more patient and understanding to yourself and others."

Gratitude

The more we are thankful for what we have, instead of focusing our thoughts on what we don't have and what we want, creates the possibility to attract more things into our lives to be grateful for. A positive mindset and appreciation attracts a more fulfilling life. Don't compare yourself and your life to anyone else's because we never truly know what inner battles others go through, despite how they appear to be on the surface.

"Be grateful for every moment in every day, because you were given a gift of life to be grateful for, so use it wisely."

Knowledge

We gain knowledge as we move through our lives, through our existence, through our education, we learn through people and our relationships. To live life understanding in more depth the nature of why things happen and looking at things with an open mind and acceptance, you gain more knowledge as to reasons why unwanted circumstances and situations happen to you or loved ones and potentially grow from the knowledge life has given you.

"Knowledge stems from many sources, not just books, there are limitless opportunities to learn and gain more insight to the purpose of life and your existence on Earth."

Gratitude Meditation

- Sit quietly for a few moments and close your eyes, relax with every breath you take in and out.
- Be aware of how your body feels, what thoughts and feelings you experience.
- Breathe in trust, peace and gratitude, breathe out tension, stress or worries.
- See a colour of your choice, breathe the light from this colour into your body, into your heart and mind, feel compassion, kindness, love and joy.
- Stay with all the magical feelings that this light gifts you and feel grateful for all the things you have in your life and your loved ones you share your life with.
- Send this feeling of contentment and fulfilment towards others, your loved ones, anyone who may be in need of some healing.
- Spread the light from within, until you feel ready to open your eyes and come back.

Live Your Dreams Poem

For all your dreams you keep within,
have courage to live them and never give in.
Even when they seem so difficult to achieve,
have faith and in time your destiny will be revealed.

Keep following your heart's desire on the path that you take,
don't let life pass you by, don't leave it too late.
Make your own choices, don't be led astray,
once on the right track, you will find your own way.

Keep pressing on to achieve the goals you set,
feel fulfilled and content, not living with regret.
So trust your own instincts, just relax and have fun,
be happy and courageous, your journey has just begun.

Goals

Set goals in life, make them achievable and achieve the unexpected. Let go and let god to all your hopes and dreams, never think that any goal is out of reach because hard work, determination and discipline will create magic in your life. It is best to keep an open mind and never predetermine the end result because this could limit your life's purpose.

"Dream hard, work hard and let the rest unfold, there is no limit to your personal success and any goal you set yourself is just a belief within reaching distance."

Inner Dreams

We have dreams within us to give us a purpose to strive for. We may have varying dreams at different times in our lives as we evolve. A dream is a thought or idea that your spirit is calling to you to fulfil and achieve, it does not want to be denied, it wants to be lived through your existence to give you gratification and excitement for life.

"Dream any dream as big as you possibly can, follow this dream through and make it a reality in your world."

Believe

Don't allow barriers, obstacles, dark skies to cloud your judgements on what you set yourself to accomplish. Put your self-belief into action and do not be swayed by doubts and insecurities. If you believe in you and believe that something is worth fighting for, whatever this maybe in life, then stay true to yourself and keep believing.

"Believe in yourself and you will succeed, don't allow doubts and fears to interfere, be awakened to your calling."

Wishing Well Meditation

- Close your eyes and relax, breathe in a little deeper and slower with every breath you take.
- Visualise a forest scene that you are walking in, all troubles forgot and just feeling a sense of serenity and tranquillity.
- In the distance you head towards a wishing well, each step you take you draw closer to it.
- Once you approach the wishing well, you reach down into your pocket and find three coins.
- With the first coin you drop down in to the well, you make a wish to let go of something that no longer serves you, something negative in your thoughts and mind.
- You now take your second coin and drop this one into the well. This time you make a wish to heal a loved one.
- The third coin that you drop into the well, you wish for something in your future.
- Once all wishes have been made, you leave the well and return to you waking state as you open your eyes.

An Angel's Whisper Poem

I started to fall, you pulled me up,
I heard a voice saying never give up.
The feelings I have had, full of doubts,
if only I could understand what they're all about.

I take a step forward each single day,
with a positive thought and silently pray.
I become stronger in faith as I'm losing my fears,
Troubles are fading, as I wipe away tears.

A spiritual journey each moment lived,
joy and happiness to receive and to give.
Light fill my soul, love found from within,
With peace and harmony a new day begins.

Prayers

There will always be a silent listener to all your unanswered questions and uncertainties. If you go within and sit with your own spirit and the spirit world who unconditionally love and support you, release all your concerns and with gratitude and trust, your prayers will be answered. Sometimes we do not always get the result we wish for but we always get what we need and we will never know of the underlying difference and significance a loving prayer can make.

"Silently or aloud, pray to your God and wait for answers to awaken within or present themselves to you in unexpected ways."

Signs

Notice signs as a way of direction and meaning in your life and current circumstances. There are no coincidences, only indicators to get your attention. Physical signs could be a particular person and a conversation you have, a song you hear, a white feather from a loved one in spirit, or it could be your inner voice or gut feeling making you listen to your heart.

"Look for the signs that come into your life, as they are telling you what you already know but have not been listening to."

Trust

Give up your thoughts of what if's and when's and allow the divine to unfold the magic within, have total trust that all will be okay. When we try to force the outcome to any given situation, we allow ourselves to get in the way and put obstacles along our path, which then can become a struggle, if we relax and go with the flow of life and not swim against the current, we can enjoy the journey and not just wait for the destination.

"Your spirit hears your doubts and fears, so surrender to the power of the divine, trusting that your prayers have been heard and will be answered."

Floating Cloud Meditation

- Close your eyes and begin to picture in your mind you floating on a white fluffy cloud.
- Feel yourself floating, rising a little higher amongst other clouds in the sky. As you just drift and float your mind is feeling more clearer, losing all sense of time and forgetting any worries or concerns.
- Allowing your mind to feel so peaceful and serene allows access to a higher mind and consciousness.
- All you can see is white from the clouds around you, you visualise the outline of an angel and feel the warmth and presence of a spiritual being.
- As your feelings and awareness gets stronger and more connected to this source, you find yourself absorbing wisdom and guidance, support for your life in this moment.
- You stay with this connection for a short while until eventually your time comes to an end and you start to drift back down on the cloud, until you reach the ground and become aware of your surroundings.

The Answers are Within Poem

When you feel you're on your own and have nowhere to turn,
don't look outside, look within and find out what you yearn.

Go deep within, what's in your heart, to hear what speaks to you,
hopes and dreams, desires and wishes, what do you want to come true?

You may not have the job you want, so why do you choose to stay?
if the relationship you're in is unfulfilling, then why not walk away?

Not enough money, or not enough time to nourish yourself with treats,
find direction and strength within to put yourself back on your feet.

Guidance

Follow the guidance from your own intuition, from loved ones in the spirit world and loved ones in your life who you respect and trust, as a listening ear may be required. We were not put on earth to have an individual existence, we are each a part of one another in some way like an extended family. Listen carefully to the guidance you receive and go forward in trust.

"Follow the guidance that your heart is communicating to you, trust your own intuition and advice from a trusted source."

Movement

For when we stay still in the silence of our own being, can we truly connect to the bigger picture and life as a whole. Allow the power of your own spirit to move and guide you through this time in your life. Wait for clarity and focus from your higher mind to direct you to the next step in your journey that will unfold the best possible outcome for your concerns and indecision at this moment in time.

"Be still, be silent and wait for the presence of God to flow through your consciousness and unlock the answer to your question."

Time

All things happen within divine timing. It is not wise to rush or dictate the result we desire in any given situation in case we alter the outcome in a less favourable way. But if we have patience, work hard, remain positive in all that we do and live in the moment, life will unfold as it is meant for the highest good, and then we are truly blessed.

"Make your time on earth count, enjoy you journey, live in the present moment, not looking back or too far ahead."

Inner World Meditation

- Close your eyes, imagine every time you breathe out you're breathing away tension and anxiety, every breath in, you breathe in healing and peace.
- Visualise a door, as you open the door you walk though it to the other side.
- This door has led you to a very special and unique place, your inner world.
- You see rays of golden light, warm and an inviting place to enable you to relax and unwind.
- Relax with warmth and harmony, compassion and peacefulness.
- As you completely close the door to your outer world, you allow yourself to fully engage into your inner world. A world where you feel safe and can experience pure love and joy.
- Allow yourself this special time to work on yourself and your happiness, feeling a sense of balance on all levels.
- When you feel you have spent enough time here you can close the door behind you and know that you can return at any time again.

Morning Sky Poem

I woke up one morning and looked up to the sky,
not a cloud or storm, insight or nearby.
Pure and clear and sparkling blue,
shining above both me and you.

Feel your dreams with all you might,
look up, reach out to your visions in sight.
Hold them within and never let go,
or free them and live them and watch yourself grow.

Each day, each week, each month and year.
know that your love will conquer all fear.
For when you see clearly, no storm to be seen,
Held you will be in this blissful dream.

Abundance

Feeling you have all that you want and all that you need is true wealth and priceless. Abundance does not mean you have the most expensive house or labels on clothes, it means you feel complete within yourself and blessed for all you have. If you are living your life feeling truly abundant you feel uplifted and positive with lots of energy and motivation. Hold onto this way of being as you are truly connected to the divine.

"To attract more good into your life, every day acknowledge all that you have to be grateful for and feel complete in every aspect of your life knowing that you are abundant."

Value

Each day wake up and value yourself as much as you value the person you love and value the most. Don't ever wait for approval from another, your opinion of you is enough and you yourself has an important part to contribute in this life. Value you yourself highly, believe in your self, do your best in life and serve your calling.

"Value you yourself highly and never underestimate yourself and how you have a positive impact on others that come into contact with you."

Transformation

As we go through life from childhood, into our teenage years and then adult hood we notice changes within ourselves but we always remain the same spirit that was and will always be. It is our human existence, our personality hopes and dreams that may evolve. We transform through life experiences and relationships. We are guided at different times and usually under different influences, have the courage to follow through any wishes you have and continually transform closer and closer to your spirit.

"When you get to a time when you want to try something different or grow out of your comfort zone it is probably drawing you for a change and transformation within."

Hot Air Balloon Meditation

- As you close your eyes visualise yourself walking down a country lane.
- You can feel the sun beating down on you, you make your way to a huge hot air balloon for you to step into and make your journey.
- You take off and gently and safely you steadily rise higher and higher, drifting above the fields and houses below, the cars on the roads, everything begins to look smaller and smaller as you continue to drift higher and higher.
- You're amongst the clouds, and drifting and floating takes you to a new place where you can shed away unwanted baggage, be free and still in your new found bliss.
- No noise, just silence, reflecting on your life at the present moment you can take the time to imagine letting go of physical and emotional stress and leaving it behind.
- When you start to return down, you begin to feel much lighter as if all the burdens you were carrying before have been lifted from you and you are now just left with an inner sense of calm and peace.

Bonds Between Relationships Poem

In life we form bonds with family, friends, colleagues and lovers,
some come and go, some stay longer than others.
Special connections made, are often hard to find,
creating precious moments and memories together over time.

Enjoying each other's company, experiencing life together,
these bonds are unbreakable and will remain forever.
Trust in one another, be kind, supportive and sharing,
through happy and sad times, always remain loving and caring.

Be grateful for your loved ones that make your life more whole
that special moment when like minds connect uniting soul to soul.

Family

We are all born into this world with a birth mother and father and sometimes siblings. We have our biological families and then there is our extended families who play many different roles to us. Our friends, teachers, neighbours, pets are our soul family. Love your family for who they are in your life and all that they are unconditionally, we all have our strength and weaknesses, no one is perfect and accept the imperfections in one another.

"Love your family, biological and extended, because although blood is thicker than water, the spirit that we ach are, is thicker than blood."

Friendships

There can be friends that share a life time with us and there are friends that walk a short distance in our path, but they each have their place in our journeys. We can learn so much from the friendship's we encounter some can be our soul mates. Appreciate the times you share, learn to let go of ones that no longer serve a purpose in your life and embrace the ever changing new friends that appear into your life.

"We have friends for a long time or short time that can leave an impression for ever, special memories made that can always be treasured."

Reward

The greatest reward will not be found from material values and possessions. It will be from success of your happiness, from the love you give and receive, the company of people in your life that share your hopes and dreams and that you can share there's also. Cherish the rewards you are granted from all the good that you put into this world and the happiness you feel from it.

"You will always receive for what you give out so the more good you do, expect to be rewarded for your time and efforts."

Candle Meditation

- Close your eyes, imagine that there is a candle flickering in front of you.
- Focus on the candle watch the flame and its changing colours as a focus.
- Imagine the candle melting away all your troubles and worries and the warmth of the flame warming and comforting your soul.
- Find healing and peace as you breathe in the light from the flame, illuminate your physical body. Clear your mind and thoughts as you breathe in the healing to balance your mental wellbeing.
- As you focus back on the candle visualise the healing from the candles light reaching out to others, your loved ones, pets, family and friends.
- Visualise us all connected as one together, supporting each other, generating loving kindness, compassion and peace.
- Allow the feelings of stillness, healing and tranquillity to create a beautiful energy and stay with this feeling as long as you need, before returning to the start, when in your own time you can open your eyes.

Unconditional Love Poem

The feeling of love comes in many different ways,
it can give you a lift on your darkest of days.
A hug from a loved one, a chat with a friend,
be there for each other, from the start to the end.

Display unconditional love, even when it's sometimes hard to do,
accepting others flaws and weaknesses, as well as yours too.
Listen with an open heart and willingly be there,
don't judge or criticise, just show that you care.

Breathe in, breathe out, fill your heart with love and light,
the feeling of joy and contentment, that is forever glowing bright.

Love

Only when you truly love yourself unconditionally, beyond the physical surface, mistakes, guilt, defeats and failures, can you begin to experience self-love and see the world and its true beauty by becoming aware of the perfection within its imperfection. Love can be found where it is not looked for in any given moment, if we can open our hearts and minds to this feeling.

"Love yourself kindly with open arms as you would love another that is dear and precious to you, see yourself through God's eyes."

Acceptance

Sometimes we may find it hard accepting things in our lives that we don't like, so by making an effort to make changes or finding a way to accept what we can't change, we then begin to live more in harmony and swim with the current of the tide instead of against the waves. When we accept everything each day for what it is, we embrace life instead of fighting against uncertainties or unwanted circumstances.

"Accept unconditionally what cannot be physically changed and make an effort to change what you feel you need to, to find contentment."

Beauty

True beauty is not what something looks like on the outside, it lies within us all and what we each represent. There is a story behind every person and the masks that we often disguise ourselves behind can hide the natural beauty of our true essence. Allow yourself to shine from the inside out and don't contaminate yourself with self-doubting thoughts, other people's opinions and past failures.

"See the beauty in you and in the beauty of life as a whole, look beneath the surface to find your hidden sparkle and the spark of the divine in all creation."

Healing Heart Meditation

- ❖ Relax and close your eyes, bring your awareness to your heart and imagine that it is a flower with lots of petals.
- ❖ You sense you heart is opening and expanding and as it does so the petals open layer by layer. Each layer represents different aspects of yourself.
- ❖ The first layer opens and your heart is open for physical healing.
- ❖ The second layer represents emotional and mental healing.
- ❖ The last layer that opens is the spiritual aspect of yourself, connecting you to your truth and higher self.
- ❖ Your heart is warming and filling with love.
- ❖ In your mind you say to yourself some inward affirmations.
- ❖ “My body, mind and spirit are in perfect balance and harmony”.
- ❖ “Any past pain, hurt or grievances are being released now”.
- ❖ “The power of unconditional love is healing me”.
- ❖ When you’re ready, open your eyes and return to your normal waking state.

Never Give Up Poem

Whatever the task or challenge you take,
is always a step forward and not a mistake.
In the journey of life and the choices you make,
are under divine guidance and in hand with fate.

If there comes a time when you feel like giving up,
change your way of thinking, keep your head held up.
Just try to keep your faith, in time you'll start to see,
The dreams you hold within your heart can be reality.

There may be bumps in the road and mountains to climb,
but trust that in time everything will turn out fine.
Keep strong and determined, overcome triumphs and
tests,
take on every hurdle and be proud that you're doing
your best.

Inspiration

As we go through our life we continually learn, grow and develop through challenges and experiences. We may be inspired to try something new or make change in our current situation and circumstances, but we are often too scared to take the leap of faith. We sometimes compare ourselves to others and wish we had more confidence. Believe in yourself, don't always reach out for others to inspire you, be the inspiration for your life and what you wish to become or do, because we each have that spark of the divine light within us.

"Allow your spirit to continually transform through various stages in your life, don't remain stagnant, instead challenge and inspire yourself. Be within your light and shine it out to the world."

Karma

It is possible to create our own karma, governed by the laws of attraction, when we do good for another and when our behaviour is positive, we create an external world that is kind to us. Like attracts like, so the people who we attract into our life and the types of relationships we have can also reflect what messages we are intentionally or unintentionally sending out to the world. However if you feel you are giving all that you can to the world and being the best that you can be and life seems to throw you difficult people and life circumstances, try not to think of this as a punishment or negative. Try to understand the lessons that can be learned and turn a negative into a positive, as you could be being tested and strengthened, so remain positive and strong.

"What you give out to the world is what you get back in return, give all you have and expect to be rewarded, give up and give in and you will limit your growth."

Hope

Hope is a powerful magnetism that attracts you to all things that are beautiful. If you can hold hope in your heart whatever is going on around you in your life and within you personally, you will be granted support and comfort from the Divine. Hope shines a spark of light through any storm and apprehensions and brings forth happiness, joy and positivity.

"Always have hope even in the dark moments of your life, because it will see you through to the light, the sunshine and colourful rainbow of life again."

The Book of Change Meditation

- As you relax with your eyes closed and make yourself comfortablc, you visualise a very old looking door.
- As the door unlocks, it's hinges creak as it slowly opens to reveal a library.
- Its empty and silent and in the corner to your right you see a small wooden desk, on this desk lies a large old book.
- You hold the book in your hands and feel a sense of wonder, you open the cover and notice it is blank inside.
- This is a book of change; it has the ability to free you from any burdens that weigh heavy on your shoulders.
- It is time to write in this book and create a story of your life that you desire, any potential changes you wish to come true, any goals and targets.
- Write down things that you no longer want in your life, the stress, worry, doubts and fears and any physical imbalances you may have.
- Replace the negative with the positive.
- When you have finished you can open your eyes and find yourself fully awake.

The Material Soul Poem

You may have a high paid job to give you a feeling of success,
have expensive designer clothing to make you look well dressed.
Own a posh flash car, to take you where you want to go,
have a luxurious home, to look good and have on show.

But can you have strength and love in your heart when life doesn't go your way,
can you have faith, acceptance and gratitude for the simplest things each day.
Are you complete within your own being, or do you look for happiness outside,
in times of need do you run to others, or can you find the answers inside.

Giving

What we give out to the world we give back to ourselves. If you give unconditional love, positivity, time and support to others etc, then expect to experience these for yourself. When we feel ungrateful and as though we are always needing something, then we are working on a different lower vibration, instead of attracting abundance in our lives by the natural law of attraction.

"When you give to others, ensure it is for the pure reason of wanting to give and honour yourself the gifts of love, happiness and time, you deserve for you."

Joy

Find the Joy in the simplest things in life. We can have physical possessions which can please our hearts for a moment, but they are only short lived. The joyous moments and memories we create have far more power and influence in our sustained happiness than anything of material value. True Joy is living our lives being with those who we care for dearly and doing what we love.

"We were not born to be unhappy we were born to live in joy, whatever isn't working in your life change it and use the power of your own spirit to be happy."

Treasure

Real treasure is not material or physical, it is hidden within each of us and when we experience those moments of joyous simplicity creating memories of happiness with those who are near and dear to us, and loving life and what each day brings, this is the treasure and gift that no money can ever buy.

"When we have flashes of completeness, feeling whole and experiencing unconditional love, it is then we have found our treasure."

Contemplation Meditation

- Close your eyes and focus on your breathing.
- Each breath in, hold for three seconds, each breath out, release for four seconds, do this until you feel more relaxed.
- Bring your awareness to your heart and feel a smile and happiness light it up, glowing warm and lovingly from the inside out.
- Focus on where your thoughts are directed and if they don’t feel happy then let them go and calm your mind to only happiness, love and joy.
- Inwardly say some positive affirmations.
- “I am happy and peaceful despite my external circumstances”.
- “I am content and abundant regardless of my material possessions”.
- “I am grateful for all the people in my life, my close loved ones”.
- “I reflect happiness and joy to the world”.
- Once you have spent enough time in contemplation you come back to the beginning and open your eyes feeling much more settled than you did before.

What Matters and What Doesn't Poem

It does not matter what job I do, where I live or car I drive,
as long I'm healthy, happy and well, I'm grateful for life and continue to strive.
The job that I have, does it please me or not,
am I following my heart or have I forgot?

If I am lead by other people and follow by their way,
I only have myself to blame for being led astray.
When I hear the inner voice I call upon inside,
it takes away my fears and doubts, I sometimes try to hide.

What does matter to me, is that I'm able to forgive and forget.
to live each day in joy, with no resentment or regret.
Not only to forgive my own mistakes, but other peoples to,
I wish for unconditional love that is pure, divine and true.

Regrets

Mistakes and regrets are a natural part of our human existence. It would be impossible to go through life without having regrets, thinking what if and how things may have turned out differently if you had made other choices. Repeated life lessons may come up until we learn to act in a way that is allowing you to learn from the past. Don't be hard on yourself learn from your past and move forward in hope for the future.

"Don't dwell in regrets there will always be new doors opening of opportunities and potential for you to embrace in the present and future."

Insecurities

We all have times in our lives when we face defeats, are hurt by another, we will have lost someone close to us we love in some form, we will have made mistakes fallen and rose again. What happens in our past is in our past. If we look back and ask ourselves what we have learned or gained positive from that experience and what can we take from it to help us in the future. Don't allow other people's opinions to impede on your confidence, what is important is that you believe in you and be proud of who you are and how you are living your life.

"Don't allow past hurtful events to fuel your future thoughts and expectations of what is to come. Gain strength and wisdom not a mind full of insecurities and negative self-beliefs."

Emotions

Emotions can consist of positive and negative. We have challenges, triumphs and heartache to enable us to appreciate joy, happiness and love. By keeping a diary of our feelings and emotions in the cycles of life we can understand ourselves more fully and be able to live more in balance and harmony. When others behaviour towards us is perceived as negative, we are given the opportunity to choose how we react and this determines our emotions, we can observe our reactions and learn from them as we move forward.

"If we learn to truly understand our self and what can influence are emotions we can learn to take control of our unique power and not allow our negative emotions to defeat us."

Moments of Time Meditation

- Relax, unwind and close your eyes.
- Visualise a house where you open the front door and go into explore.
- You take a door on your right and as you enter this room you see scenes from your past. Good times, sad times, celebrations, memories never forgotten. If there is anything in your past that still holds you back in any way then this is your time to let it go once and for all, close the door behind you and move on to the next room.
- The next room is on your left and as you enter this room, you are in the here and now, so take time to be accepting for all you have and what you have achieved, realise what matters in life and what doesn't, appreciating and giving thanks.
- You leave this room and head to a third room down the corridor. This room leads you to your future, here is the time to make any wishes, any intentions or aspirations for the future.
- You leave the house once you have finished and can open your eyes.

Make Dreams Come True

We are all born with dreams, which we want to see come true,
but you have to work hard to achieve them, and realise it's down to you.
They will always be just dreams, if you don't try to make them real,
so if you don't put in the effort, don't believe you have had a bad deal.

It's when you stay strong and determined and have faith in yourself and believe,
for if you always wait for tomorrow, you'll never begin to achieve.
So start today by pursuing, on any wishes and goals you hold,
to do your best to make come true and let your future unfold.

Creativity

There is creative side in each of us waiting to be expressed in some way possible. Some people express their creative gifts in the way of music, writing, art, sport and it can also be expressed in what we love doing in our work. Become in touch with what makes you feel alive and have passion to express your creative side that tells the story of who you are and demonstrates your talents.

"Express what you want to share to the world in which ever way you feel guided to do so, unleash your creativity hidden within."

Detachment

Sometimes detachment can be the best option, because if you are trying to force or determine an outcome to something that is beyond your control you can waste your own energy and time dwelling on this. It is sometimes best to sit back and just allow the universe to answer your prayers and provide the best possible solution to your situation. As the saying goes "let go and let god" wait patiently for the outcome that will appear in the near future and in the meantime spend your thoughts and time constructively and positively.

"We sometimes wish for things that aren't what we really need, so trust and faith are beliefs that will serve your spirit and your purpose more kindly in the end."

Discipline

To achieve something of importance to you there may be hard work involved to get the result you wish for, stay determined and disciplined to your work because things will pay off in the end. You may need to balance your time more and make compromises or sacrifices to achieve what you set out too. You may need to discipline your mind to change your thought patterns from fears and worries to positive thoughts of succeeding and accomplishment.

"Discipline is the key to achieve the miracle you aspire for, believe this is attainable and working hard for it, spread your wings and fly."

The Puzzle of Life Meditation

- Close your eyes and relax.
- Visualise yourself in a room with a large table and lots of pieces to a puzzle.
- Think of your life and all your accomplishments, all the hard work you had to do to achieve them.
- Think of the choices you made, the paths you have taken.
- As you do this, you start putting the puzzle together, joining piece by piece.
- This puzzle is a picture of your life, the people who have played a part in it, places of significance, special times and memories, all displayed in a puzzle.
- You notice some areas of the puzzle are complete but where there are gaps, these are the areas in your life that still need completing.
- You can continue you with this jigsaw whenever you return to this meditation, creating the story of your existence.
- But for now you open your eyes and return.

Shining Star

I lie awake before I sleep and gaze upon a star,
I feel it's light shine down on me, so close although a far.
It twinkles bright within my soul to give me strength within,
and feel it's spark within my heart in every day I'm living.

I thought of you as the star shining bright,
always spreading joy, happiness and light.
Remembering the special and fun times we shared,
how loving you were, how much you cared.

I know you'll still be around, just a thought and a heartbeat away,
I'm grateful for having you in my life, and the memories we shared each day.
Remembering how you were in life, generous, funny and kind,
a friend like you is forever treasured and very rare to find.

Light

The spark of the divine is within each of us. The light within, some may call this our own God, this helps to keep us strong and focused and in touch with the spirit we each are. When you are lost and in need of guidance, go within to the light that shines the way forward out of the darkness into the sunshine of happiness, into the light, into your light.

“The light within will be your compass for direction when you are going through struggles and triumphs in your life, allow it to shine within and without.”

Calling

Some may be aware of this and some may not. It is something that our spirit wants to communicate with us as we live through our journey on Earth. There is a personal destiny or purpose within each of us, it may take a life time to reach and attain or even understand this concept. It can feel like a deep hunger or discontentment that you are searching to feed. Despite having all that you could possibly want materially and having a happy life there is something missing if we don't fulfil our calling.

"Acknowledge that you have a unique calling and awaken to this, allow your spirit to guide you towards it and unfold your true purpose."

Healing Light Meditation

- ❖ As you make yourself comfortable and close your eyes, your awareness is on a shining star in the sky.
- ❖ The star is shining so brightly, beaming down on you and illuminating you.
- ❖ You breathe this light into your crown and allow it to move down in to your physical body.
- ❖ Observe it travel from your head, all the way down to your feet, relaxing you, calming you and making you have a sense of oneness and connection with the universe and all its wonderful energies.
- ❖ As you breathe out, you breathe this light all around your physical body and extend it to your aura.
- ❖ This light heals you on all levels, physically, emotionally and mentally.
- ❖ Your physical body is rested and rejuvenated.
- ❖ Your emotional and mental wellbeing is in perfect balance.
- ❖ Your spiritual connection is of pureness.
- ❖ Feeling healed you now start to awake and open your eyes.

“Live with perseverance and strength through any difficult time and challenge you face.
Live with unconditional love for everyone, regardless of gender, age, nationality, sexuality and race.
Live with gratitude for the gift of life that you have been blessed to have.
Live with compassion for every soul on earth that comes into your life and crosses your path.”

About the Author

In the summer of 2020 I was inspired to write from my heart and create a book filled with spiritual guidance, philosophy and inspiration to share to as many readers as possible who would be drawn to my words. You can read this small book from start to finish or just pick up whenever you feel the need for a lift or some guidance.

You can choose a meditation to enjoy whenever you wish to relax, unwind and heal.

The aim of this book is to help anyone going through a challenging or difficult period in their life and who needs to return to their inner strength and light, to continue along their life's path and soul's journey.

The Author of this book, Karen Parry, is a certified:
Reiki Healer and Teacher
Meditation Teacher
Hypnotherapist
Holistic Therapist
Soul Plan Readings Practitioner
Intuitive Card Reader and Medium

Telephone: 07821 584379
www.cheshirereadingsandtherapies.co.uk
karenparry79@hotmail.co.uk

www.ingramcontent.com/pod-product-compliance
Ingram Content Group UK Ltd.
Pitfield, Milton Keynes, MK11 3LW, UK
UKHW042009190726
13854UKWH00005B/2222

9 781800 312951